WHO'S WHO OF PRO SPORTS

WHO'S WHO OF

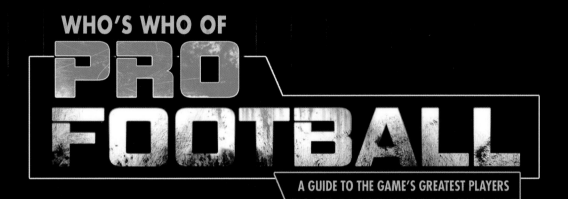

A GUIDE TO THE GAME'S GREATEST PLAYERS

by Andy Rogers

CAPSTONE PRESS
a capstone imprint

Sports Illustrated Kids Who's Who of Pro Sports are published by Capstone Press,
1710 Roe Crest Drive, North Mankato, Minnesota 56003
www.capstonepub.com

Library of Congress Cataloging-in-Publication Data
Rogers, Andy (Andrew David), 1978–
  Who's who of pro football : a guide to the game's greatest players / by Andy Rogers.
     pages cm.—(Sports Illustrated Kids. Who's Who of Pro Sports.)
  Includes bibliographical references and index.
  Summary: "Introduces readers to the most dynamic pro football stars of today and yesterday, including
notable statistics and records"—Provided by publisher.
  ISBN 978-1-4765-5715-1 (library binding)
  ISBN 978-1-4914-7608-6 (eBook PDF)
1. Football players—Biography — Juvenile literature. 2. Football players—Rating of—Juvenile literature.
I. Title.
  GV939.A1R64 2016
  796.332092′2—dc23
  [B]
                              2015002810

Editorial Credits
Nate LeBoutillier, editor; Kyle Grenz, designer; Eric Gohl, media researcher

Photo Credits
Newscom: Cal Sport Media/Manny Flores, 9, Icon SMI/Richard A. Brightly, 27; Shutterstock: David Lee,
6; Sports Illustrated: Al Tielemans, 14, Andy Hayt, cover (right), Bob Rosato, 19, Damian Strohmeyer, 4, 25,
David E. Klutho, 8, 11, Heinz Kluetmeier, 15, John Biever, 20, 26, John W. McDonough, 17, John Iacono, 23,
Peter Read Miller, 22, Robert Beck, 5, 7, 10, 28, Simon Bruty, cover (middle), 12, 13, 16, 18, V.J. Lovero, 21,
Walter Iooss Jr., cover (left), 24

Design Elements: Shutterstock

Printed in the United States of America in North Mankato, Minnesota.
042015   008823CGF15

TABLE OF CONTENTS

GODS OF THE GRIDIRON

How do fans define the greatest players in the National Football League (NFL) today? For certain, great players make great plays. Great quarterbacks throw clutch passes. Acrobatic receivers make diving catches. Tough linebackers make game-saving tackles. Powerful running backs break tackles for important first downs. Cool-headed kickers nail game-winning field goals. The stars of these plays make fans stand up and cheer. Many of these stars have etched their names in the record books. Now their names grace the pages of *Who's Who of Pro Football*.

ROB **GRONKOWSKI**

AARON **RODGERS**

GREATS

Modern-Day MVPs

When a player makes all the right moves for his team, he becomes truly valuable. Check out the list of the most valuable players (MVPs) from the past 15 NFL seasons.

Year:	Most Valuable Player:
2000	Marshall **Faulk**, running back, St. Louis Rams
2001	Kurt **Warner**, quarterback, St. Louis Rams
2002	Rich **Gannon**, quarterback, Oakland Raiders
2003	Peyton **Manning**, quarterback, Indianapolis Colts Steve **McNair**, quarterback, Tennessee Titans
2004	Peyton **Manning**, quarterback, Indianapolis Colts
2005	Shaun **Alexander**, running back, Seattle Seahawks
2006	LaDainian **Tomlinson**, running back, San Diego Chargers
2007	Tom **Brady**, quarterback, New England Patriots
2008	Peyton **Manning**, quarterback, Indianapolis Colts
2009	Peyton **Manning**, quarterback, Indianapolis Colts
2010	Tom **Brady**, quarterback, New England Patriots
2011	Aaron **Rodgers**, quarterback, Green Bay Packers
2012	Adrian **Peterson**, running back, Minnesota Vikings
2013	Peyton **Manning**, quarterback, Denver Broncos
2014	Aaron **Rodgers**, quarterback, Green Bay Packers

REMARKABLE RECORDS

Aaron Rodgers is the only current quarterback to have a career passer rating above 100. He posted a 122.5 rating in his 2011 MVP season.

Master Manning

Peyton Manning has been a leading NFL quarterback since he joined the pros in 1998. The five-time MVP is a master at directing an offense. If he sees the defense line up in a certain way, Manning might call an audible right before he takes the snap. This changes the play and gives his team a better chance for success. Thanks to this kind of decision-making, Manning has led his teams to Super Bowl appearances following the 2006, 2009, and 2013 seasons. In 2006 Manning captured the Super Bowl MVP as his team, the Indianapolis Colts, won it all.

PEYTON **MANNING**

STAT-TASTIC

In 2014 Peyton Manning broke the NFL record for career touchdown passes. He threw his 509th TD pass to Demaryius Thomas on October 19, 2014.

Graham the Great

The best tight ends are crosses between offensive linemen and wide receivers. To do their jobs, they need to be big but nimble. Jimmy Graham stands 6-foot-7 (2 meters) and weighs 265 pounds (120 kilograms). He throws booming blocks and led the entire NFL in touchdown catches with 16 in 2013. He was selected to the Pro Bowl in 2011, his first year as a starter, and again in 2013 and 2014.

REMARKABLE RECORDS

In 2011 Jimmy Graham set a new NFL season record for tight ends with 1,290 receiving yards. It was broken a few hours later by Rob Gronkowski of the New England Patriots.

JIMMY **GRAHAM**

Big Joe

Joe Thomas, offensive tackle for the Cleveland Browns, is a mountain of a man. At 6-foot-7 (2 m) and 300-plus pounds (136-plus kg), Thomas is the perfect size for an offensive tackle. Though he's huge, Thomas—like most of the NFL's best offensive linemen—rarely gets noticed. He will probably never score a touchdown. But that's OK with him. He works so that his teammates can get the glory. In 2014 Thomas was selected to his eighth straight Pro Bowl.

JOE **THOMAS**

Confident Corner

Cornerback Richard Sherman defends the field like no other player. Never shy to take on the opponent's top receiver, Sherman is known for his unique ability to back up his confident ways. From 2011 to 2014, no one in the NFL had more interceptions (24) or passes defended (70). With that in mind, quarterbacks tend to avoid throwing near him. Sherman helped the Seattle Seahawks win Super Bowl XLVIII following the 2013 season.

STAT-TASTIC

Richard Sherman takes everything he does seriously. In high school he earned a 4.2 grade-point average, which is better than an A average.

RICHARD **SHERMAN**

Powerful Watt-age

Only two defensive players—Alan Page and Lawrence Taylor—have ever won the NFL MVP. But J.J. Watt made a great case for himself with his performance in 2014. The Houston Texans' defensive end harassed quarterbacks all season, getting 20.5 sacks. Watt also forced four fumbles, recorded a safety, and returned an interception for a touchdown. His dynamic play wasn't just limited to defense. Several times Watt lined up on offense when the Texans were near the goal line. As a surprise receiver, Watt caught three touchdown passes in 2014.

J.J. **WATT**

REMARKABLE RECORDS

J.J. Watt compiled 20.5 sacks in both 2012 and 2014. No other player has ever recorded more than 20 sacks in a season twice.

Gone with the Wind

Few plays change the momentum of a game as quickly as punt or kick returns for touchdowns. Devin Hester is the best in the business. Going into the 2015 season, Hester holds the NFL record for combined kick and punt returns for a touchdown with 20. He doesn't always receive the chance to score. Fearing Hester's speed, punters often angle their punts out of bounds when they see Hester lined up to receive a kick. They know that if Hester gets loose—look out!

DEVIN **HESTER**

REMARKABLE RECORDS

Devin Hester broke Deion Sanders' NFL record for combined kick and punt return touchdowns on September 18, 2014. Sanders was a fantastic athlete and the lone Super Bowl winner to also play in pro baseball's World Series.

Feet of Strength

Being a good placekicker requires a level of confidence and consistency unique to other NFL positions. Coaches, players, and fans expect kickers to make nearly all of their field goals and extra points, which often decide outcomes of games. The Detroit Lions thought so highly of kicker Jason Hanson that they kept him for 21 seasons. Hanson scored 2,150 points for the Lions during that stretch.

STAT-TASTIC

In 2011 Jason Hanson became the first player in NFL history to score more than 2,000 points for one team.

JASON **HANSON**

Hometown Hero

The Green Bay Packers have a definite advantage playing at Lambeau Field, where every game since 1960 has been sold out. Packer fans especially enjoy watching quarterback Aaron Rodgers play there. On November 16, 2014, Rodgers broke the NFL record for consecutive passes at home without throwing a single interception. He passed New England Patriots quarterback Tom Brady's previous mark of 288. He still hadn't thrown a home interception by the end of the 2014 season.

AARON **RODGERS**

REMARKABLE RECORDS

Aaron Rodgers won his second NFL MVP award following the 2014 season. He threw 38 touchdowns and just 5 interceptions.

DREW **BREES**

A Mighty Brees

Even the best NFL passers have an occasional off game. But Drew Brees of the New Orleans Saints doesn't have them often. Brees set a new NFL record in 2012 by throwing at least one touchdown pass in 54 consecutive games. That's more than three years' worth of games. He broke a 52-year-old record set by Johnny Unitas, who threw touchdowns in 47 straight games. Brees' record-breaking throw was a 40-yard scoring strike to receiver Devery Henderson in a 31-24 win over the San Diego Chargers.

STAT-TASTIC

Peyton Manning had been the fastest quarterback to reach 50,000 yards passing in his career. He reached the milestone in his 191st game. In 2013 Drew Brees reached 50,000 yards in his 183rd game to best Manning's mark.

Crystal Ball Colin

San Francisco 49ers quarterback Colin Kaeperneck is a dual threat. He shows his value by successfully running or throwing the ball. Another of Kaepernick's amazing abilities includes predicting the future. When he was in fourth grade, Kaepernick wrote a letter stating, "I hope I go to a good college in football. Then go to the pros and play on the Niners or the Packers even if they aren't good in seven years." By February 3, 2013, Kaepernick was not only playing for the 49ers—he was their starting quarterback in the Super Bowl.

COLIN **KAEPERNICK**

STAT-TASTIC

Colin Kaepernick set an NFL record with 181 rushing yards by a quarterback in a 2013 playoff game against the Packers.

Twisted Metal

During Calvin Johnson's 2007 rookie season, his Detroit Lions teammate Roy Williams nicknamed him "Megatron." Williams named Johnson after a popular Transformers character because Johnson was known for his great size and strength. The NFL's Megatron is bent on dominating other teams as one of the most high-powered wide receivers in the game today. On November 27, 2014, Johnson caught his eighth Thanksgiving Day touchdown pass, an NFL record.

CALVIN **JOHNSON**

Chapter 2

AGED GREATS

Receiving Royalty

Nothing gets fans out of their seats like a pretty touchdown catch. Some receivers go high into the air to put points on the board. Some toe the sidelines to make scoring grabs. Some use their blazing speed to turn short passes into end zone celebrations. Here's a list of the eight receivers in NFL history to catch 100 touchdowns or more.

Receiver:	TDs:	Active:	Teams:
Jerry **Rice**	197	1985–2004	49ers, Raiders, Seahawks
Randy **Moss**	156	1998–2012	Vikings, Raiders, Patriots, Titans, 49ers
Terell **Owens**	153	1996–2010	49ers, Eagles, Cowboys, Bills, Bengals
Cris **Carter**	130	1987–2002	Eagles, Vikings, Dolphins
Marvin **Harrison**	128	1996–2008	Colts
Tony **Gonzalez**	111	1997–2013	Chiefs, Falcons
Tim **Brown**	100	1998–2004	Raiders, Buccaneers
Steve **Largent**	100	1976–1989	Seahawks

RANDY **MOSS**

REMARKABLE RECORDS

Jerry Rice holds many NFL receiving records for a career. These records include touchdown receptions (197), receiving yards (22,895), and total catches (1,549).

Legendary Leader

Don Shula knew how to coach. Shula roamed the sidelines from 1963–1995, coaching first the Baltimore Colts and then the Miami Dolphins. His masterpiece season came in 1972 when Miami went 17–0 and won the Super Bowl. To this day, Shula's 1972 Dolphins have played the only undefeated season in NFL history.

DON **SHULA**

STAT-TASTIC

In addition to coaching for 33 years in the NFL, Don Shula played for seven seasons. He made 21 career interceptions as a defensive back for the Browns, Colts, and Redskins.

Iron Man

By the end of his career, Brett Favre had set many quarterbacking records, such as most touchdown passes (508) and passing yards (71,838). He also gained respect for his outstanding durability in such a high-impact sport. From 1991 to 2010, Favre played through bumps, bruises, sprains and even a broken thumb in 2003. He never missed a start. In all, Favre started 297 consecutive regular-season games—321 including playoff games. During Favre's streak, 238 other quarterbacks started NFL games for the league's other teams.

BRETT **FAVRE**

REMARKABLE RECORDS

Brett Favre is the only quarterback to defeat all 32 NFL teams. Favre set the record in 2009 when his Vikings beat the Packers, whom he played for in 16 of his 20 NFL seasons.

With Honor

Not all football players earn their greatest achievements on the gridiron. In 2002 Arizona Cardinals All-Pro safety Pat Tillman left the NFL and joined the United States Army. Inspired by the events of 9/11, Tillman enlisted with his brother Kevin to help defend the United States. After turning down a $3.6 million contract offer to continue playing football, he served tours in Iraq and Afghanistan. Tragically, Tillman died in uniform in 2004.

STAT-TASTIC

Pat Tillman was named an All-Pro in 2000 after compiling 145 tackles, the most of any safety in the NFL that season.

PAT **TILLMAN**

Chapter 3

TERRIFIC TEAMS

The Greatest Show on Turf

Prior to the St. Louis Rams' 1999 season, Kurt Warner was an unknown backup quarterback. But when starting QB Trent Green went down with injury, Warner stepped in. His play spurred on what became one of the most successful offenses in NFL history. Speedy receivers Isaac Bruce and Torry Holt and rambling running back Marshall Faulk helped Warner's Rams score a then-NFL-record 526 points on the season. The Rams capped their season by winning the Super Bowl.

KURT **WARNER**

REMARKABLE RECORDS

The Rams were the only team in NFL history to score more than 500 points in three consecutive seasons from 1999–2001.

Killer Combos

A balanced pass-and-run attack is often the mark of a championship offense. Therefore it's no surprise that most great NFL quarterbacks handed the ball off to superb running backs. Quarterback Joe Montana won three Super Bowls for San Francisco in the 1980s with running back Roger Craig. Dallas Cowboys quarterback Troy Aikman won three Super Bowls in the early 1990s with running back Emmitt Smith. Denver quarterback John Elway and running back Terrell Davis won a pair of Super Bowls for the Broncos in the 1990s.

STAT-TASTIC

Terrell Davis ran for 2,008 yards in 1998, the fifth highest season total in NFL history.

TERRELL **DAVIS**

Strong as Steel

The Pittsburgh Steelers were the best NFL team of the 1970s thanks to an aggressive defense nicknamed "The Steel Curtain." It featured Hall of Famers Joe Greene, Mel Blount, Jack Ham, and Jack Lambert, and it was the backbone of their dynasty. During a nine-game stretch during the 1976 season, Pittsburgh quarterback Terry Bradshaw sat out with an injury. But the stingy Steeler defense allowed just two touchdowns in Bradshaw's absence. Pittsburgh captured seven division titles and four Super Bowls in the 1970s.

REMARKABLE RECORDS

In the 1974 draft, the Pittsburgh Steelers took Lynn Swann, Jack Lambert, John Stallworth, and Mike Webster. They are the only franchise to draft four future Hall of Famers in one year.

Nowhere to Run

Despite having an average offense, the 2000 Baltimore Ravens won Super Bowl XXXV. There was nowhere to run against the Ravens, who never allowed a single running back to gain 100 yards in a game all season. On the season, the Ravens' defense allowed just 970 total yards and just 10.3 points per game, both NFL records.

STAT-TASTIC

In 2014 the Seahawks' defense led the NFL in fewest points allowed for the third straight season. The only other defense to accomplish that was the Vikings' "Purple People Eaters" from 1969–71.

Ancient Rivals

One of the longest-running rivalries in all of sports belongs to the Chicago Bears and Green Bay Packers. From 1921 to 2014, they played each other 190 times with the Bears winning 93 times, the Packers winning 91, and the teams tying 6 times. With a ticket to the Super Bowl on the line, the Bears and Packers met for the NFC Championship game on January 23, 2011. Star quarterback Aaron Rodgers threw for 244 yards to secure a 21-14 Packers victory. Green Bay then went on to win the Super Bowl.

REMARKABLE RECORDS

The Bears' 61-7 win over the Packers in 1980 was the largest victory in the rivalry. Amazingly, the Packers had beaten the Bears 12-6 two months earlier in the season.

New York, New York

Most fans root for the hometown team. But for some fans, it's not that easy. The New York Jets and New York Giants play in the same state, city, and stadium. The teams only play each other once every four years because they're in different conferences, but when they do, both teams have home field advantage.

STAT-TASTIC

The New York Giants lead the all-time series 8–4 against the New York Jets.

Monsters of the Midway

The 1985 Chicago Bears had one of the greatest seasons in NFL history. With a defense featuring Mike Singletary and Richard Dent, the Bears growled their way to a 15–1 record and a Super Bowl title. They only allowed 198 points during the season. In the first two playoff games, Chicago held both the New York Giants and the Los Angeles Rams scoreless. The Bears then roared to a 46-10 victory over the New England Patriots in Super Bowl XX.

The 12th Man

During the Seattle Seahawks' home games in 2013, it seemed like there was an extra player on the field. With an extremely loud fan base, the Seahawks broke the Guinness world record for loudest outdoor stadium with a 137.6-decibel reading. The loud crowd distracted the opponents and gave the Seahawks extra energy. The defense allowed the fewest points and yards in the league during the season. It all led to the Seahawks winning Super Bowl XLVIII, the franchise's first championship.

REMARKABLE RECORDS

Seattle scored the quickest Super Bowl points ever, getting a safety 12 seconds into Super Bowl XLVIII.

WONDERMENTS

Greatest Nicknames

Best Nicknames of Today	
Name	Nickname
Marshawn **Lynch**	"Beast Mode"
Darrelle **Revis**	"Revis Island"
BenJarvus **Green-Ellis**	"The Law Firm"
Ben **Roethlisberger**	"Big Ben"
Carnell **Williams**	"Cadillac"
Andy **Dalton**	"The Red Rifle"
BJ **Raji**	"The Freezer"
Tyrann **Mathieu**	"The Honey Baddger"
Robert **Griffin** III	"RG3"
Calvin **Johnson**	"Megatron"

Best Nicknames of Yesteryear	
Name	Nickname
Joe **Namath**	"Broadway Joe"
Jerome **Bettis**	"The Bus"
Walter **Payton**	"Sweetness"
William **Perry**	"The Refrigerator"
Harold **Grange**	"The Galloping Ghost"
Reggie **White**	"The Minister of Defense"
Joe **Greene**	"Mean Joe Greene"
Elroy **Hirsch**	"Crazylegs"
Deion **Sanders**	"Primetime"
Dan **Wilkinson**	"Big Daddy"

Greatest Records

Only perfect season: The 1972 Miami **Dolphins** (17–0)
Most single-season touchdown passes: Peyton **Manning**, 55 in 2013
First player with 10,000 rushing and 5,000 receiving yards: Marcus **Allen**
Most single-season rushing yards: Eric **Dickerson**, 2,105 in 1984
Most single-season touchdowns: LaDainian **Tomlinson**, 31 in 2006
Most career rushing yards: Emmitt **Smith**, 18,355
Most career receiving yards: Jerry **Rice**, 22,985
Most career field goals: Morten **Andersen**, 565
Most career sacks: Bruce **Smith**, 200
Most career interceptions: Paul **Krause**, 81

STAT-TASTIC

Running back Marcus Allen threw six touchdown passes in his career.

Glossary

consecutive (kuhn-SEK-yuh-tiv)—when something happens several times in a row without a break

dynasty (DYE-nuh-stee)—a team that wins multiple championships over a period of several years

extra point (EKS-truh POYNT)—a play after a touchdown where the ball is kicked through the goalposts for one point or taken into the end zone for two points

field goal (FEELD GOHL)—a play in which the ball is kicked through the goalposts for three points

passer rating (PASS-uhr RAYT-ing)—a measure of the performance of quarterbacks taking into account touchdowns, interceptions, yards, and completion percentage

Pro Bowl (PRO BOWL)—the all-star game of the NFL

sack (SAK)—to tackle a quarterback attempting to pass the ball

statistics (stuh-TIS-tiks)—numerical facts or data

Read More

Frederick, Shane. *Football: the Math of the Game.*
Mankato, Minn.: Capstone Press, 2012.

Hetrick, Hans. *Six Degrees of Peyton Manning:
Connecting Football Stars.* Six Degrees of Sports.
North Mankato, Minn.: Capstone Press, 2015.

Storden, Thom. *Amazing Football Records.* Epic Sports
Records. North Mankato, Minn.: Capstone Press, 2014.

Internet Sites

FactHound offers a safe, fun way to find Internet sites related to this
book. All of the sites on FactHound have been researched by our
staff.

Here's all you do:

Visit *www.facthound.com*

Type in this code: 9781476557151

Check out projects, games and lots more at
www.capstonekids.com

Index